My Senses

Mike Jackson

Illustrated by

Jon Davis

Mum and Dad are taking us to see Grandma.

Look at the cows!

We use our eyes to see.
Sight is one of our senses.

Hello
Grandma!

We use our noses to smell.
Smell is one of our senses.

Bye,
see you later!
Listen to all the birds
singing in your garden.

We use our ears to hear.
Hearing is one of our senses.

Oooh, you've got a new kitten, Grandma!
She's pleased to see you.

We use our fingers to
touch things.
Touch is one of our senses.

These apples taste lovely!
Those are eating apples.

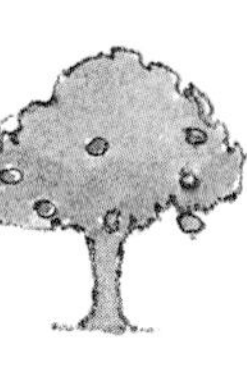

We use our tongues to taste things.
Taste is one of our senses.

Can we pick some cooking apples to make a pie?

Is this the recipe for apple pie, Grandma?
Yes, I'll put my glasses on to read it.
I wear glasses all the time.

Some people wear glasses
to help them to see clearly.

This apple
tastes sour.
We'll sweeten the apples
with some sugar.

Some things taste sweet and some things taste sour.

I've got some very cold water for making the pastry.
Don't touch the pan. It's very hot now.

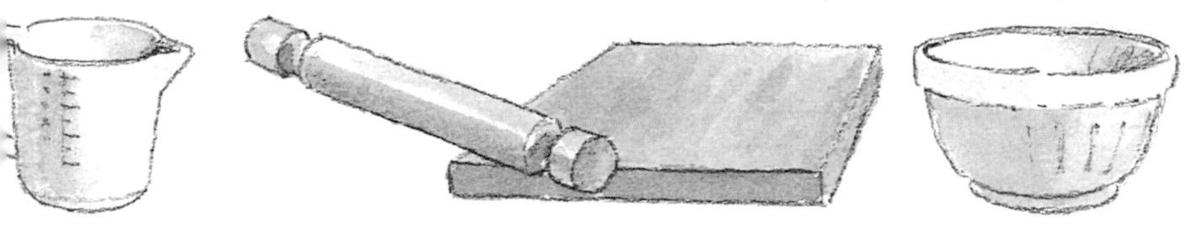

Some things feel hot and some things feel cold. We can feel things with the nerves all over our bodies.

The cooked apples smell lovely.

I love the smell of cooking.

We like the smell of
some things.
We don't like the smell
of other things.

We can hear quiet noises.

Shhh, I can hear the oven timer ticking.

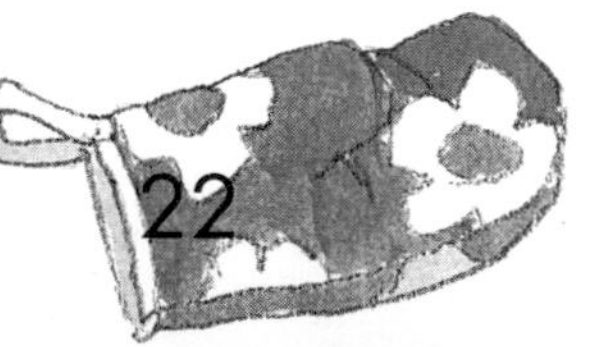

1·30
The pie is nearly ready now.
Let's lay the table!

We can hear loud noises.

The timer is ringing!

I'll get the pie out of the oven.

Hurray!

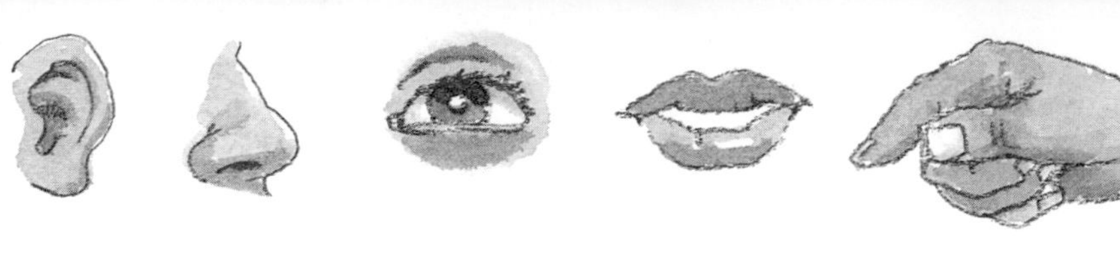

This pie looks good.

And it smells good.

We have five senses. They are sight, smell, hearing, touch and taste.

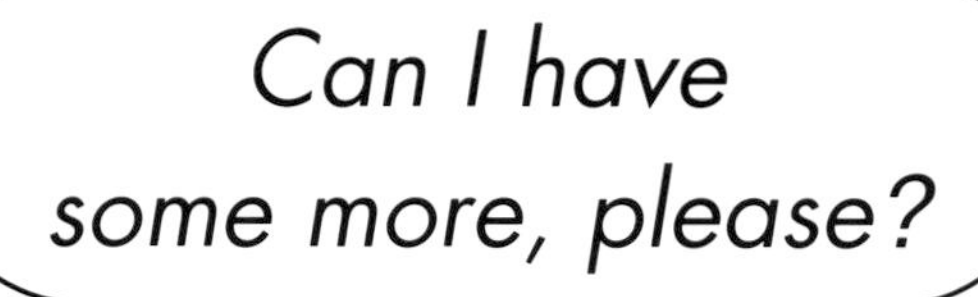
Can I have some more, please?

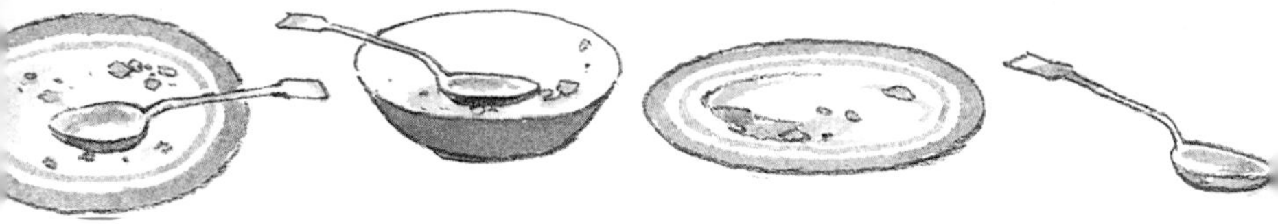

We use our senses to enjoy the world around us.

 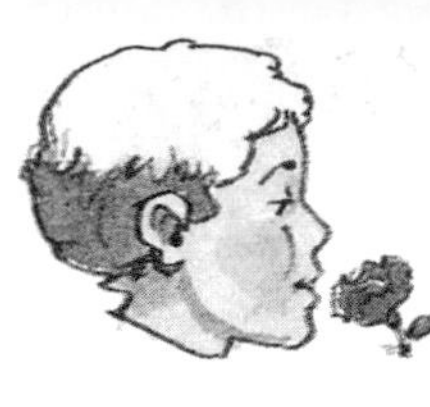  

Can you remember which of the senses we learnt about in each of these pictures?